Modern Originals

Modern Originals

AT HOME WITH MIDCENTURY
EUROPEAN DESIGNERS

by LESLIE WILLIAMSON

RIZZOLI
NEW YORK

New York Paris London Milan

Contents

Introduction

It is hard for me to believe that the humble beginnings of *Modern Originals* were in 2005. It was then that I first made a list of all the houses of my favorite architects and designers that I wanted to visit in my lifetime. I was a fan of design and had an insatiable curiosity to see how these people—whose work I loved, lived with, and was inspired by—lived themselves. The list was rather innocent at the time, just an afternoon's musing on future travels. What has come to pass between then and now perhaps requires a recap.

In 2006, after being dismayed to find that no book on these homes existed, I decided to begin photographing them myself. I was taking a break from my photography career, and was considering leaving photography altogether, but the idea of photographing these homes reignited my interest in taking pictures again. So I began. By the time I had shot two houses, I had a set of criteria as to what I was looking for in terms of houses. Although I was exploring design, interiors, and architecture, I was also exploring these designers' lives. Their homes—whether these designers were living or their home was preserved as a museum—became an in-depth portrait of the designers themselves. I worked slowly, shooting when I could afford to, and after four years I had enough for a book. In October 2010, *Handcrafted Modern: At Home with Midcentury Designers*, my first book, was released, featuring fourteen homes of designers in the United States.

The response to *Handcrafted Modern* was a delightful surprise. When I was shooting it, this work felt very personal and I shared it with only a handful of friends. With the book's release, I learned that I was not alone in my love of these designers and how they lived. After a short break, I began planning the next round of photo shoots in Europe. I have been asked why Europe, but to my mind this was never a question. The original list is worldwide, so my intention was always to continue on photographing these homes, wherever they may be. Furthermore, somewhere along the line I realized I am building a library of these designers and how they lived for future generations. This gave my work a purpose that I never could have imagined. It has changed me in every possible way. Or maybe it has made me exactly what I was meant to be. I am not sure at this point, but I love where it has taken me.

So this brings us to late 2011, when I began planning which homes I would include in *Modern Originals*. I started with my original 2005 list and quickly found that many of the houses I had dreamed of photographing, if they were not house museums, no longer existed or were unavailable to be photographed. There were numerous reasons for this: theft, death, illness, and government bureaucracy, being the main ones. This realization had a strange effect on me: it made me painfully aware that the clock was ticking on even the homes that seemed secure and, oddly enough, made me full of faith that the right homes would come to me for the European book.

The criteria for the homes in *Modern Originals* remained virtually the same as for *Handcrafted Modern*. I have listed them below, but keep in mind that there are exceptions to all of them. I am guided first and foremost by my love of these designers' work—and being an artist, I went where inspiration led me.

1. The home has to be intact with the person still living there, and preferably designed by the architect/designer for him- or herself or inhabited by him- or herself for many years and customized.

2. If the person is no longer living, and the house is a museum, it must be preserved as it was when the designer was living there, with their personal effects still in the home.

3. I photographed the homes as I found them, within reason. I would only move objects if they were distracting and/or obscuring the larger whole, and I have been known to dust and vacuum on occasion.

4. I shot for two full days at most houses with a few exceptions based on the size of the residence (Le Corbusier's Cabanon is only 145 square feet—it did not take two days to photograph), or the occasional scheduling issues with house museums or homeowners.

5. I used only natural light or the lighting of the house, so the photographs faithfully reflect how it would be for the person living there.

Modern Originals was photographed over two trips, each of about two months in duration. I traveled alone and shot alone except when I had a guide or translator. It was the most wonderful adventure! There is no other way to put it, but it was also tiring, and very unpredictable. I would love to say that I had it all scheduled beforehand and just traveled from north to south in an orderly fashion, but that was not the case. For that reason, I have sequenced the chapters in the order that I photographed the houses so you could see just how much European hopscotch I was playing—France, Sweden, Czech Republic, Vienna, Finland . . . you get the idea. The majority of the book—ten houses—were photographed on the second trip, so much of the time I would fly in, shoot a house, and fly back out. This travel is not for the faint of heart (or body) but I have never been so happy or felt so in line with what I was meant to be doing on this planet—I absolutely loved it.

As with *Handcrafted Modern*, themes and patterns emerged as I photographed. Some were just my own quirky obsessions. For example, I became very obsessed with old-school telephones. The one sitting on Alvar Aalto's desk was my favorite because it was dove gray and the receiver sat vertically, but Renaat Braem had a fascinating intercom system throughout his home where the phones had no dials, just one small round button (pg. 211). Braem's home was also full of the customizations I love so much. One of my original interests in seeing these designers' homes in person was to see how they would solve little everyday problems that arise in a house—things I would never think to improve, but a brilliant designer would. I mention a couple of these in Braem's chapter, but my favorite was right inside his front door. He was constantly having architectural plans delivered and his mail slot was rather elaborately customized to receive them.

There were larger themes that felt like an invisible thread connecting one house to the next. During my first shoot at Robin and Lucienne Day's house, I became enamored with a ceramic tile of a butterfly on a corner wall in

the living room. Paula, their daughter, shared that this piece was a gift from family friend and artist Rut Bryk, who was Tapio Wirkkala's wife. The second house I shot was Carlo Mollino and, as you will see from his chapter, butterflies play a big role in his apartment—they are literally everywhere. I knew that butterflies symbolized transformation and reincarnation, but Fulvio Ferrari, the curator at Casa Mollino, told me that in Greek, the word *psyche* means butterfly and soul. After that, as butterflies continued to show up in the houses, I found it reassuring. I took it as a sign that the home was supposed to be in the book because the designer's soul was still there. After all, in many ways that is what I am searching for in these homes. Interestingly, in the three houses where the designers were still alive—Němec, Aulenti, and Sabattini—I did *not* spot a butterfly. Also a good sign!

My interest in bookshelves continued and this time it was everyone's dedication to Le Corbusier that I noticed. It was very clear that the two major influences for all these designers were either Alvar Aalto or Le Corbusier (I nicknamed them the "Granddaddies"). This made sense considering the time when these designers were working. However, in the case of Bruno Mathsson, who collected Aalto press clippings (pg. 104), the inspiration for his home, Södrakull, traced back directly to a trip he made to the Eames House in California.

The links between *Handcrafted Modern* and *Modern Originals* are obviously very strong. I have been asked often what differences I saw between the European homes and the American ones. That is a question I will leave to the scholars and you. My approach is at its heart a very humanistic one. Yes, I love and admire these designers' eye, talent, and individuality, which are reflected in their homes, and this book undoubtedly explores that. But the very best part of this project for me is "meeting" these people as human beings through being in their home and learning about their everyday lives. If I had not visited Aalto's home I would never have known what a wonderful abstract painter he was. Finn Juhl's home was full of art, but it is a small, threadbare, hand-embroidered pillow in a side room that I still wonder about. Was it a sentimental keepsake? I am absolutely overflowing with questions I would have loved to have asked Gae Aulenti. As I mention in her chapter, she passed away a month after I photographed her home and was not there when I shot. I did meet her during my initial visit to see her apartment, and she made a strong impression on me. Even as I photographed her home, I jotted down questions about her artwork because it was obvious there is a story behind each piece. One piece made out of wood slats turned out to be a map of fishing routes in the Marshall Islands that she brought back from a trip. But I long to know more. Why did she bring it home with her? Was it a gift from someone? Spending time in her home made it impossible not to sense her strong personality.

The idea of a Modern Original seems to perfectly describe Gae Aulenti, but then again it describes all these architects and designers—each living his or her own life and creating work according to his or her own aesthetic compass. I thought that when I went to Europe I would be looking at the roots of Modernism through these designers' homes. Although that was there, it is the individuality of each of these people that was the deeply lasting impression. They were all gloriously themselves.

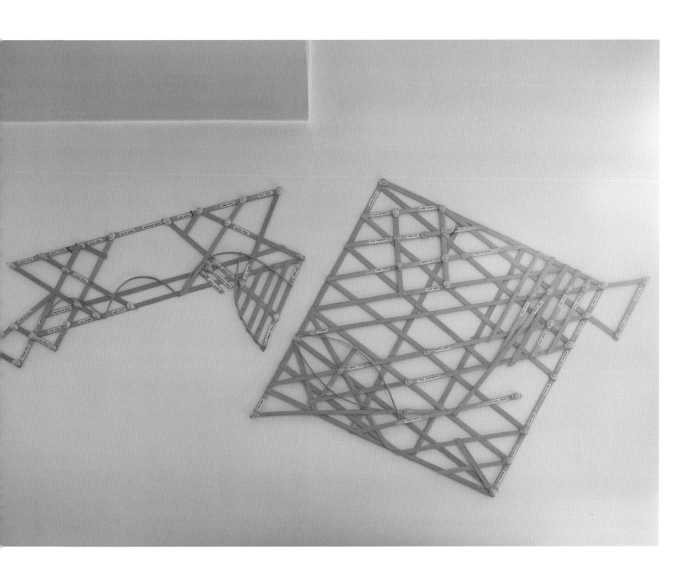

Robin & Lucienne Day

CHICHESTER,
UNITED KINGDOM

What is it about "design couples" that fascinates us so? There is something compelling about two people whose life and work are inextricably bound by love and creative endeavor. Of course everyone thinks of the Eameses when this topic comes up but my mind always goes to the United Kingdom's Robin (1915-2010) and Lucienne (1917-2010) Day. Together they are credited with transforming postwar design in Britain, and yet his furniture and her textiles are beautifully separate and distinct. One does not outshine the other, but when they did collaborate, there is an obvious harmony.

The Days' story sounded like an enchanted one to me. He a furniture designer, she a textile designer who met at a "hop" at London's Royal College of Art in 1940. It was love at first sight. They married, designed, set up their design studios in their fabled home on Cheyne Walk in London, had a child, and worked side by side in their respective careers for their entire lives. In 1999 they moved to the cathedral town of Chichester for retirement and lived out their lives here. Although both passed away in 2010, their daughter, Paula, welcomed me into their home, which remained in relatively the same state as it was when they were alive.

The basic aesthetics of their London home had been reinterpreted in Chichester and all the elements—glass shelves, curtains, etc.—had been resized to fit this smaller house. The living room was divided in two, with one half anchored around the brick fireplace by a set of Robin's Forum sofas (1964) and a pair of chairs. An ornate Baroque clock face sits on the mantel next to a piece that resembles plumbing, and next to the fireplace sits a set of handmade bellows by Robin. In the other half of the living room, floor-to-ceiling shelving houses books, a fold-down desk, and collections from their travels, all carefully arranged. My favorite pieces were one of Lucienne's silk mosaics, a piece of Lucie

Rie pottery (which on closer inspection had been broken and carefully glued back together by Robin), and a portrait of Lucienne painted by Henry Carr.

Through the door into the kitchen appeared the first bit of Lucienne's textiles—her Graphica design—as kitchen curtains. The dining room is another mix of both Robin and Lucienne's work. One of her silk mosaics, *The Castle and Other Stories*, takes place of pride on the wall. The dining table is surrounded by an upholstered set of Robin's iconic Polypropylene side chairs (1963) and a Hille credenza. As I headed up the stairs I chuckled as I noticed a curious piece of foam attached to the beam. Robin put it there after hitting his head one too many times. But Robin's sense of humor was in evidence all over the house. At the top of the stairs is his bedroom, which is simply furnished—single bed, his Festival chair (1951), an impressive collection of the *Alpine Journal* (he was an accomplished outdoorsman), and a desk. Standing on the windowsill is an odd sculpture of a figure standing with its hand on its hip. Except when I looked closer I realized Robin had merely mounted a piece of wood root he found on one of his walks onto a base. It is probably my favorite thing in the house. Lucienne's bedroom, by contrast, is filled with heirlooms from her family. On the dressing table are her mother's tortoiseshell dressing-table set, and on the facing wall sits an ornate dark wood chair she had re-covered with her Cockaigne fabric. The last room I shot was the guest bedroom high at the top of the stairs. I was fortunate enough to also stay the night here, and snuggling down under a duvet covered in Lucienne's Black Leaf design, it was hard not to feel lucky to be able to experience the Days' home as they would have. In the morning I woke to the sounds of the Chichester Cathedral bells and doves cooing on the roof. This is what Robin and Lucienne woke to every day, I thought. Wonderful.

Carlo Mollino

TORINO,
ITALY

It is hard to know where to begin when talking about Carlo Mollino (1905–1973). He is one of the most provocative, influential, and enigmatic architects and designers of the twentieth century and yet that description barely scratches the surface. He also happened to design a race car for Le Mans, invented new instruments for airplanes, developed new techniques for downhill ski racing, and over his lifetime produced a personal library of erotic photographs in which he controlled every element of the image to stunning effect. All of these pursuits in another man might have produced a hideous hodgepodge of uninteresting artifacts but Carlo Mollino produced a body of work simultaneously divergent in subject and yet consistently sinuous and theatrically beautiful.

I was already a diehard Mollino fan when I learned that one of his apartments in Torino had been opened as Museo Casa Mollino. I vowed to experience it firsthand. Upon arriving, I learned that he never lived in this particular apartment. Mollino kept four residences around Torino, and this was the last apartment he took (in 1960). He referred to it as a "warrior's house of rest." Fulvio Ferrari, the house's curator, told me that it is believed Mollino was creating a sort of pharaoh's tomb here, where he would accumulate all his desired earthly possessions to bring into the afterlife. After hearing this theory, the rooms took on a deeper meaning.

The entryway is a virtual indoor garden. Flowers bloom off the blue-and-white tile floor and Venini glass chandelier. The red and gold velvet curtains are multifunctional—serving as both window coverings and backdrops for Mollino's photographic setups. A white marble table (1964) next to the front door was designed by Mollino especially for this apartment but otherwise there are few stand-alone Mollino pieces. His furniture was designed for specific interiors and therefore are one-offs and extremely rare.

The main living area is divided into three rooms just off the entryway through a chinoiserie-inspired screen. One enters into a central sitting room with two chaises—a Thonet and Corbusier, respectively—sitting next to a pair of huge clamshells that flank the terrace door. Two small brass dog figurines stand like sentries on watch. To the left is a smaller sitting room with a large pastoral nineteenth-century etching covering the entire far wall and an oddly small Louis XVI-style fireplace, designed by Mollino, with a figure of a woman sitting inside. Ferrari said this figurine always sat in this spot. The dining room is on the opposite side of the central sitting room with a Mollino-designed marble table surrounded by Saarinen tulip chairs and a Gianfranco Frattini–designed fringed lamp tucked in the corner. A black cabinet with a butterfly on its door hides a secret bar.

The kitchen is conveniently located across the hallway. The long galley-style kitchen could accommodate one person at best. Sitting near the stove is an original chestnut-and-oak chair that Mollino designed for the Casa del Sole apartments in 1953. This is hands-down my favorite Mollino chair, so I treated myself to a sit-down break. Down the hallway is the bathroom, which is tiled in a red-and-gold Vietri tile and features magazine cutouts of familiar starlets, all scantily clad, hanging on the walls.

Across the hall, the last room looks out onto the River Po and is etched on my memory because of the army of butterflies and leopard print on its walls. Butterflies symbolize the soul and immortality, and the hypothesis is Mollino designed this room as his "tomb" for the afterlife. The satin-swathed bed has an Egyptian motif with snakes carved into its design. On the opposite wall is an elegant layering of mirrors and a bust of a woman. I glanced up and was surprised to find another cast, this one an ample female derriere, hanging close to the ceiling. On second thought, I was not surprised at all. If this was to be Mollino's tomb, it fit perfectly with his legendary love of women. He would undoubtedly have been surrounded with them in his afterlife.

Studio
Achille
Castiglioni

MILAN,
ITALY

I believe there are some rare and wonderful places in this world that carry the energy of the people who spent time there, even long after they have departed. I know it sounds New Age-like, but this has been my experience. Achille Castiglioni's studio in Milan is such a place.

When I first walked through his studio door at 27 Piazza Castello, I did not know that Castiglioni (1918–2002) was known for his curious and playful nature. I knew him as one of the masters of twentieth-century design. With his brother, Pier Giacomo, he designed some of the most iconic and influential furniture and objects of the twentieth century, most notably the Arco lamp (1962, Flos), and a group of Marcel Duchamp Readymade–inspired pieces including the Mezzadro and Sella stools (1957, Zanotta) using a tractor and bicycle seat, respectively. In 1962 the brothers moved their design practice into this studio, and after Pier Giacomo's untimely death in 1968, Castiglioni continued to work here for the rest of his life—some forty years. Today, this four-room L-shaped studio is still intact and run as a museum by Achille Castiglioni's family.

The entrance leads to a short book-lined hallway that connects the two front rooms, which face the street, to the rear rooms of the studio. I immediately went right, toward the green 40/80 chair (1999), which Castiglioni designed with Ferruccio Laviani, and continued through to the meeting room. Castilgioni's long Leonardo table (1940) sits at the center of the meeting room, surrounded by a variety of chairs, including Castiglioni classics. In front of the window rests a grouping of objects that catches my eye: a conversation of design greats—an Eames bentwood leg splint hangs on the wall, two of Castiglioni's Sella stools stand in front, and an Aalto brick sits on the radiator.

The "mirror room" is filled with examples of Castiglioni's own work and his famous found object collection. It is said that when he lectured, he would show up with a "Mary Poppins bag" full of objects from this collection and create his lecture around them. When we opened a cabinet, objects tumbled out. I cringed, but no one else appeared concerned.

The largest room in the studio was originally the main workroom and is filled with wooden drafting tables, Diabolo ceiling lamps (1998), and the majority of Castiglioni's design archives in numbered boxes along the far wall. Castiglioni's daughter, Giovanna, calls this "the heart of Studio Castiglioni." I peeked into a few boxes and saw original drawings with Castiglioni's corrections in pink felt-tip pen. Along the back wall, a bulletin board holds newspaper clippings, cards, and drawings from his friends, and photographs from past advertising campaigns. Many of these were images of Castiglioni himself, and it began to feel as if every time I looked up from my camera, my eyes met his somewhere in the room. I felt like Castiglioni was encouraging me.

At this point there was just one last room to explore: the Prototype room. When Castiglioni was still working here, visitors were not invited into this room. Cardboard cylinders are stored over the doorway so walking in resembled moving through a tunnel. On each tabletop sit various examples of his work throughout his career, large boxes filled with prototypes climb up each wall, and the ceiling drips with examples of his lighting designs, including my favorite, the Taraxacum (1960). I glanced up to see Castiglioni peeking at me again out of an old Flos ad on the back wall. Before I could hold back, I lay down on the floor so I could see all of his wonderful lighting from below. I usually try to maintain a sense of professionalism on my shoots but I could not stop myself. I could sense the joy Castiglioni felt for his work within these walls. That was the feeling Castiglioni left here: absolute, unbridled *joy*. And even though I heard footsteps coming toward the door, I did not rush to get up—I was having too much fun photographing Castiglioni's ceiling. I suspect he would have approved.

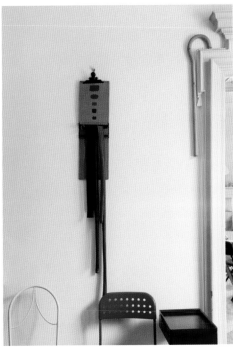

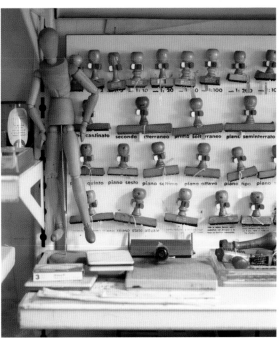

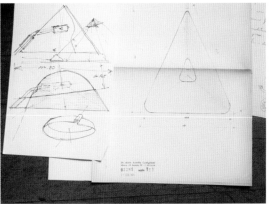

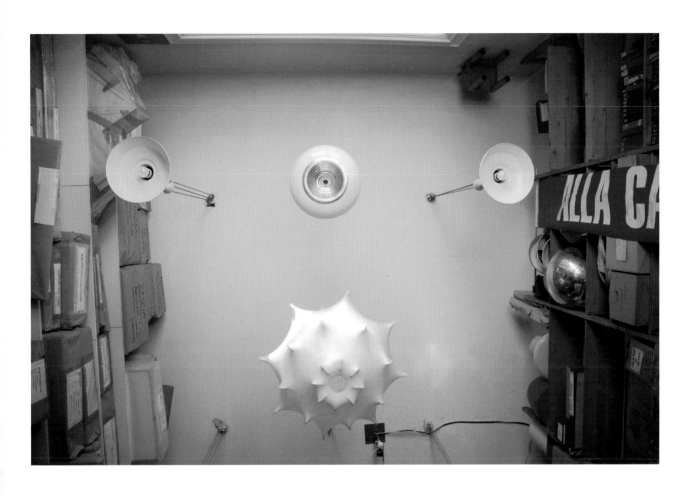

Werkstätte Carl Auböck

VIENNA,
AUSTRIA

I am not one to covet things in the houses I shoot, but when I was photographing Walter Gropius's home for my first book, I fell in love with a leather-wrapped rock on his desk. This was a paperweight by Viennese designer Carl Auböck. When I began to work on this book, Auböck was at the top of my "research" list. Although his home was no longer intact, the Werkstätte is still in the family and making products in workrooms that have been in continuous use since it was established in Vienna in 1906.

Originally founded by Karl Auböck I as a metal shop specializing in Wiener Bronzen, his son Carl Auböck II (1900–1957) took over in 1926 and developed the visual style for which they are still known today. Apprenticed in the workshops at an early age to learn the family craft and schooled at both the Academy of Fine Arts in Vienna and at the Bauhaus under Johannes Itten, Carl's modern design style gained world recognition after World War II, most notably in 1954 when he won four gold medals at the Triennale di Milano. The Werkstätte has continued to be passed down through the family, to Carl III in 1957, who continued to design new products and open the company to international collaborations, and now to Carl IV and Maria Auböck, Carl III's children.

The building on Bernardgasse that houses the Werkstätte has four floors occupied by Auböck family workrooms, offices, and apartments. The original workshops sit on the first floor and are comprised of a main workroom, polishing room, patina room, and an archive/showroom. The largest space is the main workroom with three double-sided workstations along the right side and two larger tables and a corner devoted to material storage along the left. Although the workrooms were quiet when I was shooting, each workstation had a focus of its own and the raw components of Auböck products were sitting in piles, waiting to be transformed—horn, bamboo, gourds, and brass of every conceivable thickness sat amid the tools that had been in use for generations.

Just through the polishing room with all its machinery was the patina room. Carl IV had been working here when I arrived, and as I entered the acrid smell of the acid bath still hung faintly in the air. The container for the acid bath is a thing of beauty, with a brass handle on its lid and a kaleidoscopic rainbow of chemical erosion down its sides. In front of the window sat a selection of rocks intended to become my favorite Auböck product, the leather-covered paperweight. The rocks are still collected from the banks of the Danube where Carl II first collected them in the 1940s. I looked through them all rather carefully and quietly chose a favorite. It doesn't hurt to dream.

As I was heading into the archives, Carl mentioned there was a basement that had been locked for years and I was welcome to shoot there. I could not believe my ears ("locked basement" equals dream come true for me), but I managed to stutter out a "Yes, please," and we headed down. After cutting off the lock (no key could be found) he flipped on the lights and began rooting around to see what was on the dusty shelves. The room was mostly storage but after a moment I heard Carl say "Hey! There it is!" Apparently an original cast for a design was sitting on a shelf waiting to be found.

The last room to explore was the archives, and unsurprisingly, the shelves were full of exquisite objects. It made my heart ache a little. An example of my favorite rock sat amid various versions of forks, knives, and other intimate objects of daily life that Auböck specializes in. There were even Carl Auböck clothing hangers! I felt that feeling creeping up on me again—like back in Gropius's house. So I did the only logical thing: I went back to the patina room, picked up my favorite rock, and handed it to Carl. I had to order my very own rock wrapped in leather, a balm for my covetous heart.

Le Corbusier

ROQUEBRUNE-CAP-MARTIN, FRANCE

The first time I heard about Le Corbusier's Cabanon—his retreat in the small town of Roquebrune-Cap-Martin in the south of France—the story sounded unbelievable. According to legend, Le Corbusier (1887–1965) had worn out his welcome at his friend, designer Eileen Gray's house, by stripping down to his birthday suit and painting explicit murals on the walls. Corbusier and his wife, Yvonne, loved summering in the town though, so they then struck a deal with the owner of the restaurant L'Etoile de Mer, Thomas Rebutato, who was Gray's next-door neighbor. In exchange for designing four summer cabins for Rebutato, Le Corbusier could build a small dwelling for himself on Rebutato's property. It sounds like an urban legend, does it not? This is not what one expects to hear about a man commonly thought of as one of the most important architects of the twentieth century and a pioneer of Modernism. But it is all true.

Le Corbusier (born Charles-Edouard Jeanneret) was not only a prolific architect, but also a furniture designer, painter, sculptor, theoretician, and urban planner. Before I saw his Cabanon, I equated him with white austere buildings, concrete, and ascetic spaces, which is not to say that I did not like his work. I just did not think of him as a warm Modernist. He referred to a house as "a machine for living in"—a concept that always struck me as rather depressing. When I first saw his one-room log cabin in a book, there was a modesty and humanity about it that touched me. And the fact that this was the only structure he built for himself gave me pause. Maybe I had misjudged Le Corbusier? I had to experience his Cabanon for myself.

I planned my visit very carefully: I would shoot in August at the height of the summer holiday, so I could experience his cabin as he would have. Looking in the front door, the narrow entry hall is emblazoned with one of Le Corbusier's infamous murals and at the end is a wall of colorful wooden pegs. My guide mentioned that the spacing of the pegs was based on Corbusier's Modulor

system of proportions, and then she offhandedly said that the bottom center peg was level with Le Corbusier's belly button. Of course I immediately had to stand at that peg to see where my belly button was in comparison. This simple act bestowed two lovely discoveries. The first was that Le Corbusier was much taller than I had thought. The second was that his pencil marks remain on the wall marking the original measurements.

My first glimpse into the main room did not reveal many surprises. I had looked at it so many times in different photographs that it felt familiar. The 145-square-foot room is outfitted with a built-in bed, washbasin, bookshelves, table, and wardrobe, all made by craftsmen in Corsica and shipped over. The moveable furniture in the room consists of wood boxes, used as chairs, and a low drawer on wheels that doubles as a seat. I noticed that when his wife would be in bed, she was in the unfortunate position of putting her head right next to the toilet. She took care of this with a red curtain that still hangs there today. Le Corbusier preferred to sleep on the floor. My favorite details are the clever ones that are only revealed when experiencing a space in person—the hidden towel bar in the slender space between the wall and the upright that holds the wash basin, the shutters that are half painting / half mirror to reflect the sea back into the cabin, and the drop ceiling that holds extra storage. As I shot, the summer heat began to rise and all I could think was, no wonder those wooden clothes pegs are at the entrance. Rumor has it that the moment Le Corbusier would arrive, he would strip down to his skivvies and hang his clothes on the wooden pegs at the entrance. And for a moment, in that oppressive heat, it seemed like the perfect way to pay tribute. Thank goodness I came to my senses.

Bruno Mathsson

VÄRNAMO,
SWEDEN

After shooting Bruno Mathsson's home outside of Värnamo, Sweden, I was struck by the odd impulse to look up the population of Värnamo. I could not get my head around how such innovative work could come out of such a rural area. Maybe this reaction to rural life reveals my twenty-first-century urban bias. Mathsson (1907–1988) was simply an innovator, and would have been no matter where he lived. He came from four generations of cabinetmakers, and his fascination with designing furniture that was both functional and inventive began early and was self-propelled. Never formally trained, his education consisted largely of a fortuitous arrangement giving him access to the library of Sweden's Rohsska Museum of Arts and Crafts. By 1930 he had designed his first chair, the Grasshopper (1931), which defined the visual language I have come to think of as uniquely Mathsson. Although he is largely known as a furniture designer, he also designed architecture projects in and around Värnamo for a span of ten years.

In 1964–65 Mathsson designed a permanent residence for himself and his wife Karin on a lake outside of Värnamo. They called the house Södrakull ("south hill") and it is still kept largely intact by the heirs of Mathsson's business partner, Henry Thelander, who run Bruno Mathsson International today. Henry's son, Dan, drove me out to the house for my first visit, and frankly, from the street the house looks rather nondescript. Walking into the living room, however, is a different story: windows run the width of the house and give the most sublime view of the lake. Mathsson designed every piece of furniture in the house with a couple exceptions. Books on subjects from Japanese mythology to Henri Matisse to romance novels run floor to ceiling along two walls, and all the seating is oriented toward the view. The floor plan is a basic open rectangle with the center of the house containing the kitchen and bathroom. There are no solid interior doors (save for the bathroom), just accordion partitions. A sea of green glass mosaic tiles flows underfoot throughout and picks up the green accents from the outside, making the rooms feel like an extension of the landscape.

Dan left me to shoot for the day and I took the opportunity to sit in Mathsson's fuzzy Pernilla 3 chair (1944) and listen to the house. All I heard was the sound of wind in the trees. Mathsson's collection of vinyl LPs—mostly classical—sits next to his chair baking in the direct sun. The dining area is simply furnished with a Mathsson table and two cane chairs (an early design), a Hans Wegner pendant light overhead, and a riot of color and pattern thanks to the use of Josef Frank's Aralia textile as drapes. All the curtains were drawn open when I entered the house, but these were closed. Yet, the light from the ceiling made the space an illuminated box. Mathsson had designed the roof of the central part of the house to be translucent, bringing light into what would have been an otherwise dark central kitchen. Brilliant.

Beyond another accordion door sits the office and bedroom. The office is dominated by a huge drafting table and a desk. I assume there was once a chair in between to serve both, but it must have gone missing. The industrial lamp that hung over the drafting table reminded me of the one at Alvar Aalto's home office, and as I was perusing Mathsson's books, I noticed news clippings sticking out of the Aalto books. Bruno collected press clippings on Aalto. Isn't that intriguing?

The bedroom is furnished with merely a bed, a wall of closets, and some drawers under the windows. Atop them sits one of Mathsson's hats, making it seem like he had just walked in from a long day at the office. But, apparently, he rarely worked at the office in Värnamo. He worked in this house most of the time. And why not? With the sound of wind and the view of the lake, I cannot think of a place more inspiring to create.

Joseph Němec

BRNO,
CZECH REPUBLIC

Architect Joseph Němec (b. 1924) is virtually unknown in the United States. In fact, he is not very well known in his home country of the Czech Republic either, but while researching this book, a friend in Prague, Adam Štêch, shared a picture of Němec's living room with me and from first glance I knew I had to shoot his house for this book. Němec spent most of his career at the Moravian branch of the National Institute for Reconstruction of Historical Cities and Monuments, and his work revolved mainly around reconstruction projects in Brno. From 1963 to 1968 he designed and built this home for himself and his family—much of it with his own two hands.

Upon my entering the house for the first time, the strict geometry of the architecture gave way to a surprising mix of curved forms and organic textures. We arrived with the agreement of Němec merely showing us his house. Thankfully, Adam had accompanied me and could act as interpreter (Němec speaks only Czech and German). After introductions, a quick tour, and an explanation of my book, Němec gave me permission to "take a few pictures" for it.

The glassed-in entryway is paneled in mahogany with a burst of metalwork in the corner holding coats and a collection of canes. A built-in bench has a metal claw jutting from it, which holds Němec's keys in its clutches. Just beyond the glass door are two rough carved circular wood sculptures, both by Czech sculptor Miloš Vlcek.

The living room was the room I fell in love with from Adam's photo and it did not disappoint. Mahogany, brick, and a riverstone-inlayed floor set off the avocado-green couch, which Němec designed especially for this room. A mezzanine-level dining area overlooks the living room and, out the window, the hills over Brno. The more I photographed, the more details I discovered.

Near the ceiling are many little surprises. In the corner above the fireplace, another Vlcek sculpture—this time an owl—is perched high up on a ledge, and below it in a nook in the wall is a small bust of a man peering out.

I was just hitting my stride photographing the house when Němec told us he had an appointment, so I quickly packed up. We were invited to return the next day for a few hours. We arrived the following morning promptly at 10:00 a.m. to see three sets of glasses and a bottle of wine on the dining table. We must start the day with a toast of Moravian wine, Němec informed us. Thank goodness I had eaten breakfast!

Through the swinging door in the kitchen, I saw the first of the circle motifs that would carry on in each of the three bedrooms. Němec built the house to be oriented to the sun for most of the day, and these circles symbolize the sun in each room. In the kitchen, the circle is in the form of a chalkboard, which Němec used for his grocery list (cola, a cleaning product called Cilit, and butter). Heading down the hallway toward Němec's bedroom, I noticed that inlayed stones are in the wall here, this time as long thin rectangles. His bedroom, lined with forest-green walls and a rust-colored built-in bed/couch, has another wood sculpture, this one by František Brzica called *Splitting the Atom*. It emerges vertically into the center of the room as a sort of divider. Each bedroom has a unique riverstone sun inlayed into its wall. One even integrates pieces from Němec's beloved medal collection.

When I finished, Němec looked at me with this huge smile and uttered his first word in English: "workaholic." I blushed. Adam had left early and with him went our communication facilitator. Plus, I had never shot so fast in my life. It must have looked like I was working hard, but in reality, there was not an ounce of work in it for me. It was pure pleasure—the pleasure of discovering a hidden gem.

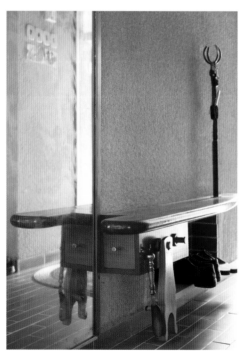

Roland Rainer

VIENNA,
AUSTRIA

Furniture design has been a gateway to all good things for me. So although Maria Auböck was the first to mention Roland Rainer's name to me, seeing his Stadthallen-Stuhl chair (1952) for the first time made me fall in love with his work. Roland Rainer (1910–2004) is best known as an architect, but he was a true polymath: urban planner, teacher, photographer, writer (he wrote, photographed, and designed twenty-seven books), furniture designer...he did it all. When I first rang the doorbell to the home he designed for himself and family in the mid-1960s in Vienna, I knew of nothing beyond his furniture design and architecture. Because of my lack of German language skills, I had only the most basic information about Rainer's career. His daughter, Johanna, who lives in the house today, filled me in on all these details. Johanna grew up in this house and—although she made a few alterations to the kitchen and bedrooms in 2010 (she is an architect herself)—the house and its contents remain much as they were when she was growing up there.

The architecture is so understated that I barely noticed it from the street. A low one-story brick house sat amid pine trees, ivy, and a sprouting brick walk. The entry area is a pared-back, minimal space, comprised of a bench, chair, and two partitions that separate it from the living room to the left and Rainer's office to the right. Johanna uses his office now, but it is still full of Rainer's library, conference table, and a set of those lovely Stadthallen-Stuhl chairs.

Entering the living room for the first time, my eyes went directly to two circles—an Eero Aarnio Ball chair (1963) and a round window that peered outside to a reflecting pool. The living room has two distinct halves: one sunken and the other on ground level. The sunken portion looks out to the deep backyard and had a wraparound built-in couch and shelving unit. At its center sits a freestanding Kaare Klint Safari chair (1933) and a low Rainer-designed square table. Rainer used white ash throughout the house for all the cabinetry, built-ins, and the few pieces of

freestanding furniture he designed for the house. This choice creates a calming consistency throughout—a continuous sea of white ash, dark wood ceilings, and walls of windows offering glimpses of the green outdoors. Rainer's favorite seat in the house is here, in the living room, gazing out at a particularly magnificent tree.

The dining room is simply furnished with a table Rainer designed and chairs of unknown origin. The wall separating the kitchen and dining room is double-sided storage, complete with a window to pass hot food through from the kitchen. These cabinets are still full of Rainer's original black-and-white Arabia Kilta dishes and a set of Josef Hoffman-designed crystal—given to Johanna's parents as a wedding gift.

Around the corner from the kitchen is a long hallway, which originally led to two small bedrooms and a master bedroom and bath. Johanna had converted these rooms into one master bedroom, but retained the original cabinetry, lighting, and bookcases. As I was setting up for a shot under one of the skylights I was struck by the geometries—circle light fixture under square skylight. Then in the master bath, I noticed it again—square white tile and square mirror. Suddenly I was seeing circles and squares everywhere. I asked Johanna if there was any significance, and she said, "No story that I know of...sorry!"

The last thing to be shot was a good exterior. Again, circles and squares—in planters, in the cutouts for trees growing through roofs. The shapes were precise, not an afterthought. This could not be my imagination. I headed over to shoot the living room's round window from the outside, and as I turned a corner there it was—a triangular-shaped greenhouse! Seeing the circle window, square reflecting pond, and triangle greenhouse all sitting in a happy threesome, I felt strangely connected to this place. Maybe there is no story, but it felt like Roland Rainer was winking at me.

Alvar Aalto

HELSINKI,
FINLAND

Alvar Aalto (1898–1976) is easily one of the most prolific and influential architects and designers of the twentieth century. I have loved his work for so long, I cannot pinpoint what first brought me to his humanistic approach to Modernism. His work always just spoke to me. So much so that it was an absolute must to include in this book the Helsinki home he designed in 1934 for himself and his family. But even now, I am surprised by my reaction to photographing it. I thought I was well acquainted with what I would find here—I had seen pictures of these rooms for years—but photographing Alvar Aalto's home felt like a revelation. I attribute some of this to my learning more about Alvar's dynamo first wife, Aino (1894–1949), who was a trained architect herself. This home was a design collaboration between the two. Officially, Alvar Aalto was responsible for the architecture and Aino for the interiors and landscape, but I find myself wondering where the lines blurred.

Until I was standing in front of the house, I had not noticed that the facade materials articulate the two different purposes of the house: the right side, which holds the studio, is solid whitewashed brick, and the left side, which contains the living spaces, features warm wooden slats around the roofline and second floor. As I walked into the living room for the first time, all the reasons I loved this house flooded my mind. The living and dining rooms flow into each other and large windows—overgrown with vines—make the back patio an extension of the living space. The living room is filled with Aalto's Artek furniture and lighting with a few notable exceptions: a grand piano, an early metal prototype tobacco table that Aalto designed but was never produced (it proved to be too expensive), and a Poul Henningsen folded paper and wood lamp, which was made as an experiment and given to Aalto as a gift. Planters, teeming with life, sit atop radiators, which run below the windows from the living room into the dining room.

The dining room is my favorite room for all the personal details that it still holds. Built-in storage holds a set of Aino's glasses for Iitala, and another credenza along the living room wall—added by Aalto's second wife, Elisa—has a hidden compartment for the extra leaves of the dining table. My favorite chairs in the house are not Aalto's designs, but ornate Venetian wood chairs brought home as a souvenir from Aino and Alvar's Italian honeymoon in 1924. Overseeing all this is an amusing sculpture of Aalto, rendered by his friend Alexander Calder. The door at the rear of the dining room leads into a modest utilitarian kitchen, which is still used today.

The family's personal quarters are on the second floor: four bedrooms and a bathroom that centered on a communal living area complete with fireplace. In the bathroom are two round sinks originally designed for Aalto's breakthrough Paimio Sanatorium project in 1932.

The double-height home studio takes up the right side of the house and was accessed through an entry off the front door but Aalto would enter each day through a large sliding wood door that connects the main workroom to the living room. This large workroom is simple, with worktables filling the space and examples of Aalto's own abstract paintings lining the walls. The paintings are all unsigned because he saw them as a part of his design process. Although he had a private office up a small flight of stairs, Aalto preferred to work at the corner desk in this communal workroom. His private office did have one feature that he would use on occasion, though: a set of stairs that led to the upper-level balcony would provide an escape route from unwanted visitors and difficult clients.

I found myself musing on this escape scenario quite a bit after I photographed the house. The home exudes such familial warmth and life that it is easy to imagine Aino and Alvar commiserating over who needed to be "escaped from" at the end of a long day. I imagine them giggling about it.

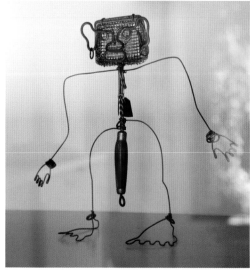

Finn Juhl

CHARLOTTENLUND,
DENMARK

When I first started this project, if asked to describe Finn Juhl's furniture designs in one word, I would have said "happy." It seems trite to me now, but I always thought of Finn Juhl as the happy midcentury Danish furniture designer. With his swoopy shapes and playful colors, Juhl's designs always had a lightheartedness that I appreciated, but this characterization made me take him less seriously. I realize now that I completely sold the guy short—but being in his home changed that. Although best known for his furniture design, Finn Juhl (1912–1989) originally trained as an architect and first made his name designing interiors—most notably the United Nations Trusteeship Council Chamber in New York (1952).

In 1942 he designed a house for himself in an affluent suburb of Copenhagen. The architecture of the house is surprisingly modest and unassuming: merely two white pitch-roofed wings connected in the middle. Upon entering, a small seating area with Juhl's low Japan chair (1958) looks out a wall of windows to an expansive garden. To the left is the open-plan living room for which the house is best known. I had seen this room so many times in photographs, but I was not prepared for its visual impact—it is a composition in coral and blues with a sneaky pale yellow ceiling.

Juhl's original goal for this house was to design it and everything used in it, and although he did not attain this goal, each room unfolds as its own precise composition of color, furniture, objects, and art. The monumental Chieftain chair (1949) stands as a sentry in the living room, surrounded by at least ten more examples of Juhl's furniture, including his Poet's sofa (1941), designed for this house, and a prototype brass reading lamp tucked away in the far corner. I became enthralled by his collection of art, full of Danish (and a few French) modern masters, most of whom I did not know. Of the forty-five drawings, paintings, and sculptures in the house, I counted eight paintings by

Vilhelm Lundstrøm alone, including the portrait of Juhl's common-law wife Hanne Wilhelm Hansen above the Poet's sofa. A Jean Deyrolle abstract painting above the bedroom fireplace ended up being among my favorites, as were the two Erik Thommesen wood sculptures.

I found the art moving me through the space. It was as if Juhl was leading my eye where he wanted me to go. The Lundstrøm portrait of Hanne, with its blues, led me into the blue sitting room, beyond which was the dark, sensuous green and yellow dining room. The Judas table (1949), with its brass inlays, and the Egyptian chairs (1949) were the focus here. Quietly tucked in the corner of the dining room was one of my favorite furniture details: a teak shelf from the credenza had a brass plate that extended over the radiator—a very elegant hot plate.

The master bedroom sits at the end of a short hallway off the dining room. It contains the furniture one would expect—all designed by Juhl—with one exception: there is a large dining table in the middle of the room. I never found out why it was there, but I like to imagine Juhl conducting meetings in his pajamas.

Passing back down the hallway toward the front door there was one more room to explore: Juhl's office. I plopped down in his Office chair (1965) for a brief moment and caught sight of another beautiful abstract painting. I smiled because it was placed so it would be directly behind the front door when it was opened. No one but Juhl would ever see it unless he or she was sitting at this desk. Artwork should be bought because you love it and clearly this one, Juhl did. I walked up to see who the artist was, expecting another unfamiliar Danish name. It read "Georges Braque"—easily the most recognizable name in his collection. And it hangs behind the front door.

Gae Aulenti

MILAN,
ITALY

My life was first touched by Gae Aulenti (1927–2012) on a visit to the Musée d'Orsay in Paris. I was nineteen years old, it was my first trip to Paris, and the Musée d'Orsay, recently transformed from train station to museum by Aulenti, was one of the highlights. Years later, when my interest for furniture design was in its early full bloom, I stumbled upon her designs and in particular her lighting. I was fascinated. Her lighting sent my imagination to other worlds—each piece was a creature from its own planet.

Trained as an architect, Aulenti's career began at the influential design magazine *Casabella* and moved fluidly from there. Architecture, furniture design, stage design, academia, architectural theory, installation art—she touched all these disciplines, and in the process became one of the few women to excel in the postwar Italian design world. I was fortunate enough to get a personal introduction to Gae through the friend of a friend and found myself entering her home/office on the Piazza San Marco in Milan. Our first meeting was very short. I was there all of twenty minutes but the impact she and her apartment had on me was very strong. When she showed me into the living room, she waved her hand around nonchalantly as if to say, "Here it is, take it or leave it." I walked away that first day with one word stuck in my head to describe her apartment: sexy. Not in the va-va-voom way, but the strong, confident kind. Take it or leave it? I would take it, thank you very much.

Five months later, as I was preparing to photograph Aulenti's apartment, I received an email a few days before my visit saying that Aulenti would not be in town for my shoot but I was still welcome. Rather disappointing, but nothing to do except go forward.

The apartment/office where Aulenti had lived and worked since 1973 is a building on the Piazza San Marco, which she remodeled to connect to an apartment in the building behind it. Entering the apartment through the office I first noticed the staggering number of books that line the walls (complete with their own numbering system). This large living room is separated into a main seating area, two smaller seating areas to the sides, and a scaffolding staircase that leads up to a mezzanine and sunroom. Most of the furniture is Aulenti's own design: April armchairs (1971), a Springa sofa (1965), and her wonderful lighting, including the Pipstrello (1965) and Ruspa (1968) lamps, sit around the room. The couch, however, is a notable exception; it is not designed by her but re-covered in a wildly patterned textile that she had collected. A Roy Lichtenstein limited-edition rug dominates the largest wall of the room with a sculpture of the Lady Justice in front, and the women depicted in each bear a striking resemblance to each other. Each grouping of art in this room tells a story. My favorite sat in a makeshift bar on Aulenti's Sanmarco table (1984). Two figures—one joyously dancing and the other clutching her head in pain—made me chuckle. Was it a commentary on the pleasures and sorrows of drink?

Beyond a doorway at the rear of the living area lies the galley kitchen and dining area and, just beyond, Aulenti's bedroom. Bedrooms are innately our most private space and this felt doubly true of Aulenti's. Although it was modern in its design, I sensed a softness and vulnerability here the moment I walked in. The mint-green canopy bed is covered in girlish red rosebud sheets. Across from the bed hangs a large drawing of a domestic scene of women. Aulenti had this drawing commissioned based on her favorite Degas from the Musée d'Orsay, *La Famiglia Bellelli*.

A little more than a month after my visit I learned that Gae Aulenti had passed away. When we met, she mentioned that she had been ill and when she was not there for my shoot, I hoped she was on the mend. Alas, that was not the case. But her home was so vibrantly alive with her personality, I feel like I know her, if only in a small way. And for that, I will always be grateful.

Lino Sabattini

BREGNANO,
ITALY

I was not that familiar with Lino Sabattini's work before I received an email with a link to a video clip on him. But after repeated viewings—I would rewind and fast-forward, trying to see the wonderful details of his home—I was on a mission to include him in this book. After a bit of patience and persistence I found myself driving toward Lake Como with the director of that film clip, Luca Mangiarotti, who was kind enough to serve as my guide and interpreter for the day.

Sabattini (b. 1925) is best known for his designs in silver but he worked in other metals as well as glass and ceramics. Completely self-taught, his break came when Gio Ponti wandered into his metalworking studio in Milan in the 1950s and liked his work so much, he published an article featuring Sabattini in *Domus*. Sabattini's career took off. He served as the director of Christofle in Paris from 1956 to 1963 and went on to establish his own design studio and factory in Bregnano, Italy, where he designed for companies including Rosenthal and Christofle. The home that he designed for himself is located a short distance from his former studio/factory.

Giada and Silver, Sabattini's two dogs, were the first to greet us, bounding down the driveway of his modern two-story home, which he designed in the early 1970s. Inside, shiny ecru lacquered furniture, designed by Sabattini, dominates. Custom pieces are in nearly every room. The main living room has three separate seating areas and examples of his work in silver, ceramics, and glass are mixed with other pieces of art and cover every surface. Above the fireplace hangs a Bernard Heiliger relief for Rosenthal and in a corner to the right is an Alexander Calder print, two ceramic plates by Nanni Valentini, and his own silver and green glass pieces from the 1980s. The large dining table is in the same ecru lacquer with a precise silver leg detail at the corners. Castiglioni's Arco lamp and an Albini wicker chair pair perfectly with all of Sabattini's silver designs on the sideboard and table. He peeked in on me at this point and caught me leaning over the one-of-a-kind silver bowl and tray on the dining table. He then walked over and casually opened one of the drawers of the sideboard to reveal that it was filled with examples of his silver jewelry. My eyes grew wide and before I knew it, he had opened a few more drawers, all just as overflowing as the first. It seemed as if every drawer and cabinet was filled with beautiful examples of his work—cutlery, flatware, dishes, you name it.

Beyond a set of doors are the kitchen and another small dining table, fully set with Sabattini-designed flatware and dishes. The kitchen is not big or flashy, just perfectly proportioned with the most exquisite chestnut wood cabinetry and detailing.

The second floor holds a central seating area around which the bedrooms are anchored. A massive wall of storage is the backdrop for more of Sabattini's low-slung couches, a Le Corbusier chaise, and another piece by Alexander Calder—this time a light. My favorite bedroom holds a modest single bed and small fireplace surrounded by more of Sabattini's ceramics. The print above the fireplace bears a striking resemblance to Sabattini himself. He told me I was close—it turns out it is a portrait of his mother by artist Rufino Tamayo.

Winding back down the stairs to the basement I found myself in the heart of what served as an informal archive. It was packed: one room for larger pieces and three smaller rooms filled with silver, glass, and ceramic pieces, many of them one of a kind. Tucked under the staircase on the wall hangs a wooden cutting board set with two knives and a cheese plane dangling from the bottom. Sabattini lamented how two of the knives had gone missing. I agreed, but it was a thing of beauty even with them missing. He designed it so when all the utensils were in use, it would still be a beautiful sculptural object. I admired how exacting and well thought out this piece was. It was much like his home—meticulous and effortless all at once.

Renaat Braem

ANTWERP,
BELGIUM

renaat braem architekt PRIVE BUREEL

Taking the taxi to Renaat Braem's home in the suburbs of Antwerp, I realized I might not recognize the exterior of his house, even if I was standing in front of it. I had become obsessed with the interiors after I saw the house in *World of Interiors* years ago, but the look of its facade had completely flown out of my head. The house, at first glimpse, caught me by surprise with its architectural restraint. Although little known outside of his homeland, Renaat Braem (1910–2001) is considered Belgium's leading Modernist architect and was an apprentice of Le Corbusier in the mid-1930s. In the mid-1950s he designed this house for himself and his wife, graphic designer Elza Severin. In 1999, Braem left the entire house and its contents to the Belgian government, and after a meticulous restoration, the house is exactly as it was when the Braems lived there.

Although the house's facade had escaped me, the front door was etched in my mind—it read "Renaat Braem Architekt" with separate buzzers for his residence and architecture studio. The front door opens to reveal a central staircase that looks like a shaft of light leading up to the various floors of the house. On the ground floor is Braem's double-height architecture office, with the second floor serving as the living quarters, and the third floor as the private rooms. It was Braem's architecture office that I had been pining to shoot and in particular his collection of wood artifacts from his travels. Every type of wood object imaginable—from Dutch shoes to a branch from a pine tree (pinecones included)—had been meticulously composed and hung on the wall behind his desk. His staff sit down a flight of stairs on the lowest, subterranean level. Across from their desks are a large table for meetings and a bookshelf filled with material samples and brightly colored file storage (which turned out to be customized with colored tape, an X-Acto knife, and a sometimes shaky hand).

The second floor is divided into a lower "evening" sitting room and an upper "day" living/dining room, with a small galley kitchen off to the side. No other word properly describes the evening sitting room except "sexy." It is warm and organic with animal hides, wood walls and flooring, a gray-brick fireplace, and a screen of plants climbing to the ceiling in front of the window. All the furniture—Noguchi lamps, Borsani D70 Divan, Jacobsen Egg chairs—were chosen especially for this house, the only exception being a Thonet rocker that moved with the Braems from their old apartment. Next to a built-in Braun stereo is another careful composition of natural curios collected on Braem's travels. Coral, sand dollars, a tiny Day of the Dead skeleton, a blowfish, and even a petrified iguana are all carefully tied with string and pinned to a grasscloth board.

The upper living room is bathed in light from two walls of windows that look out to the yard and the park beyond. Another Borsani chair, this one a mustard P40, sits near the Braem-designed dining table surrounded by Jacobsen Ant chairs. The white and primary-color-accented galley kitchen was one of my favorite rooms because of its tiny efficiency and Braem's built-in solutions for his under sink storage (on wheels!) and drawer cutting board.

All the way at the top of the stairs is the private floor with master bedroom, bathroom, and a roof terrace that during my visit was awash in rain. The simplicity of the bedroom surprised me. Because the wood cabinets were all built-in, this room was virtually furniture free, except for the bed. I noticed some odd, plastic numbered drawers across from the foot of the bed and peeked inside. Every receipt and map used from their travels, down to receipts for Perrier and peaches in the South of France, were stored here. One of my most beloved discoveries from photographing this house was the Braem's love of exploring the world that was in evidence all over their home. But to see that they even kept such minutiae as keepsakes just warmed my heart. I could have looked through those drawers for hours.

Acknowledgments

It takes many people to make a book like this a reality and all are important. First and foremost, of course, are the designers and architects themselves, their families, foundations, and caretakers.

A heartfelt thanks to Paula Day, Fulvio and Napoleone Ferrari, Giovanna Castiglioni and the Castiglioni family, Carl Auböck IV and Maria Auböck, Foundation Le Corbusier, the City of Roquebrune-Cap-Martin, Christine Coulet, Dan Thelander and Bruno Mathson International, Joseph Němec, Johanna Rainer, Mia Hipeli and the Alvar Aalto Foundation, Line Marie Lærkholm-Bengtsen and the Ordrupgaard Museum, Gae Aulenti, Nina Artioli and Vittoria Massa, Lino Sabattini, Jo Braeken, and the Flemish Heritage Agency.

A special thanks to Dung Ngo and Charles Miers at Rizzoli, Meera Deean for her copy editing prowess, Adam Brodsley and the wonderful team over at Volume, Inc., for designing a simultaneously beautiful object as well as the book I envisioned when I began. Thanks to Dirk Hatch and Lightwaves Imaging in San Francisco for being so great about how wildly picky I am about the look and color of my images and to Adam Thorman for helping make every image in this book as beautiful as I intended.

The planning and traveling that were necessary for this book far exceeded anything I have done in my life and I had a lot of help. There were many people who shared contacts, made introductions, acted as interpreters, made pledges of financial support and even acted as drivers and an extra set of hands when needed. Friends, friends of friends, and the occasional stranger (but now a friend!) offered their couches and extra rooms for me to stay and helped make this book not only a reality but also an amazing journey. I am deeply grateful for all your generosity and support. It was an integral part of bringing this book to life. Many thanks to Adam Štěch, Gianluca Mangiarotti, Hugo Macdonald, Karen John, George Beylerian, William Smolan, Marco Velardi, Alessandro Saccon, Maurizio Beucci, Alberto Ricci, Marie Gorvild, Jakob and Sophie Reese, Pontus Pyk, Unn Knape, Anders Stjernström, Harald Ekman, Manfred Werner, Sara Garcia, Omar Cabbabé, Shak Khan, all my Kickstarter supporters, and especially Dave Morin.

To my close friends and relatives who are always there for me and even more so when I am working on a project of this size. Your friendship and support throughout this process mean the world to me. I love you all. Vicki Sykes, Cletus Williamson, Pete Jost, George McCalman, Manuelita Rangel-Sosa, Michele Janezic, Janet Pullen, Maria Moyer, Cathy Bailey, Robin Petravic, Mariah Nielson, and Monika Stengert.

And most importantly, a massive thank-you to Mary Beth Phillips—my London home base and number-one go-to for support while I was in Europe. Throughout this entire book process, when things seemed a bit overwhelming, you helped me figure it out. I am so grateful for you and your friendship. You are the best, MB!

Houses You Can Visit

The following homes are open to visitors:

Alvar Aalto House
Website: http://www.alvaraalto.fi/aaltohouse.htm
Email: riihitie@alvaraalto.fi
Riihitie 20
00330 Helsinki
Finland
+35 8 09 48 13 50

Studio Achille Castiglioni
By appointment only.
Website: http://www.achillecastiglioni.it
Email: info@achillecastiglioni.it
Piazza Castello 27
20121 Milano
Italy
+39 0 28 05 36 06

Le Corbusier's Cabanon
By appointment only.
Website: http://www.roquebrune-cap-martin.com/visites-accompagnees

Finn Juhl House
Finn Juhl's house is part of the Odrupgaard Museum.
The house has limited open times so check with the
museum website for details.
Website: http://www.ordrupgaard.dk
Email: ordrupgaard@ordrupgaard.dk
Vilvordevej 110
2920 Charlottenlund
Denmark
+45 3 96 41 18 3

Museo Casa Mollino
By appointment only.
Email: casamollino@fastwebnet.it
Via Napione 2
10124 Torino, Italy
+39 011 8129868

Renaat Braem House
By appointment only.
Website: http://braem.onroerenderfgoed.be
Menegemlei 23
2100 Antwerp-Deurne
Belgium

First published in the United States
of America in 2014 by
RIZZOLI INTERNATIONAL PUBLICATIONS
300 Park Avenue South
New York, NY 10010
www.rizzoliusa.com

© 2013 Rizzoli International Publications
Texts and photographs © 2013 Leslie Williamson

Editor: Dung Ngo
Design: Volume Inc., San Francisco
Copy editor: Meera Deean
Production: Susan Lynch

The Aalto House is owned and maintained
by The Alvar Aalto Foundation.

The Le Corbusier Cabanon is a work of
Le Corbusier. © 2013 Artists Rights Society
(ARS), New York / ADAGP, Paris / F.L.C.

The Finn Juhl House appears courtesy
of Odrupgaard Museum.

The Renaat Braem House appears courtesy
of the Flemish Heritage Agency.

The Studio Museum Achille Castiglioni
appears courtesy of the Achille Castiglioni
Foundation. © Achille Castiglioni Foundation.

ISBN-13: 978-0-8478-4223-0
Library of Congress Control
Number: 2013950489

Printed and bound in China
Distributed to the U.S. trade by
Random House, New York
2020 2021 2022 / 10 9 8 7 6